LEO & DIANE DILLON

RAP
A
TAP
TAP

HERE'S BOJANGLES— THINK OF THAT!

SC
NEW YORK
MEXICO CITY

This book was originally published in hardcover

by the Blue Sky Press in 2002.

ISBN 0-439-56066-7

Published by Scholastic Inc. SCHOLASTIC and associated logos are

trademarks and/or registered trademarks of Scholastic Inc.

20 19   14/0

Printed in the U.S.A.   40

First Scholastic paperback printing, September 2003

Designed by Kathleen Westray and Leo & Diane Dillon

TO BON AS ALWAYS

Also for Bill Robinson

and Aaron Douglas

who created great art

through adversity

and who inspired

this book

There once was a man who danced in the street.

Rap a tap tap—think of that!

He brought pleasure and joy to the people he'd greet.

Rap a tap tap—think of that!

He didn't just dance, he made art with his feet.

Rap a tap tap—think of that!

He danced past doors; some were open, some closed.

Rap a tap tap——think of that!

He danced past folks in fancy clothes.

Rap a tap tap—think of that!

He danced through a place people called the skids.

Rap a tap tap—think of that!

He danced through crowds of laughing kids.

Rap a tap tap—think of that!

His feet fairly flew as he tipped his hat.

Rap a tap tap—think of that!

He briefly paused to pat an old cat.

Rap a tap tap—think of that!

He danced rain or shine, in all kinds of weather.

Rap a tap tap—think of that!

People listened each day for his toe-tapping clatter.

Rap a tap tap—think of that!

He danced many rhythms that were seldom the same.

Rap a tap tap—think of that!

Dance was his passion, and it brought him fame.

Rap a tap tap—think of that!

Bojangles, Bojangles, that was his name.

Rap a tap tap—think of that!

AFTERWORD

BILL "BOJANGLES" ROBINSON (1878—1949) is known as
the greatest tap dancer of all time. His fame has reached
mythic proportions. He had charm and charisma
and, it was said, "He talked with his feet."
His rhythms were so intricate and fast it was impossible
for other dancers to repeat some of them.

During the Great Depression of the 1930s, Bill Robinson
was the highest paid black entertainer.
He shared his wealth with less fortunate friends
and neighbors through those hard times.

Bill Robinson performed shows on Broadway
as well as in famous clubs around the country.
He formed revues that appeared in vaudeville,
and he danced in several films, including
four with the child star Shirley Temple.

On May 25, 1989, Congress declared that day
(which was his birthday) as National Tap Dance Day
in Bill Robinson's honor.